The Book of Joel

Compiled by Don Peery
Benicia Poet Laureate
2014 -2016

The Book of Joel: All Rights Reserved

Poems by Joel Fallon, First Benicia Poet Laureate, 2005 - 2008

Introduction and commentary ©2018 by Don Peery
Poems © 2004 – 2016 Estate of Joel Fallon

Published by Benicia Literary Arts
Benicia, California www.benicialiteraryarts.org

ISBN # 978-0-578-43134-5

Produced by Benicia Literary Arts, which encourages reading and writing in the community by producing events, creating a community of writers and readers, encouraging their development, and publishing works of high quality in all genres.

Design and layout by Don Peery
Edited by Mary Eichbauer and Don Peery
Proofreader, Sherry Sheehan
Cover design by Tom Stanton and Don Peery

This book may not be reproduced, transmitted, or stored in whole or in part by any means, including graphic or mechanical, without the express consent of the publisher except in the case of brief quotations in critical articles and reviews.

Contents

Forward	v
The Child	1
Young Man at Sea	11
The Soldier	21
Snapshots of Life	35
Opinion Pages	53
The Humorist	69
Love Poems	93
On Poetry	111
Endings	123
Afterword	141
Alphabetic Index of Poems	143

Foreword

It was a First Tuesday poetry reading, and Joel Fallon was holding court. The small library conference room was filled to capacity, only one chair open at the back of the room. I paused at the door. "Come in and have a seat," he said. As I did, he looked down at the paper before him and began to read in a resonant voice that filled the room. It was a poem, and he was its master. He finished to light applause, turned to his right and invited the next poet to read. I was entranced.

The poets continued to read around the table until they got to me. He asked me to introduce myself and asked whether I had anything to read. He knew nothing of my poems, but drew me out with his obvious interest. I felt as though I had found a friend, and as it turned out, I had.

This was 2005, and Joel had just been appointed the first Poet Laureate of Benicia, California. The people in the room were members of the Benicia First Tuesday Poetry Group (BFTPG) which he had founded by inviting local and area poets to "get together once a month to share their poetry." The mood was open, relaxed, and inviting. Any who came could bring their treasured poems before the group regardless of style, content, or skill. He encouraged us, mentored us, and by example, helped us to improve our poetry and presentation skills. First Tuesday poetry readings were events to look forward to, his presence a pleasure to be savored.

Joel was a force of nature. He wore his persona easily, being friendly and outgoing to everyone. He was a prince of a man and I willingly became his loyal subject.

To his memory, then, I humbly submit this book, *The Book of Joel*.

Joel Fallon

Skulls

Experts see skulls through
the lens of their specialization.

An object of sculptural beauty
adapted by evolution,
a communications portal,
a filing cabinet, an air intake portal and so on.

Experts are correct within the focus and tiny aperture of
their special lens.

A skull is all that and more:
Tabernacle, basilica, torture chamber, puzzle box
and more and more.

Each skull is different, each the same.

Observe – here on the left – the skull of Jesus, son of Joseph
and on the right – the skull of Mohammed, son of Abdullah.

No! Wait!
It may be the other way around.

San Francisco street scenes circa 1940, from Google Pics

The Child

Joel Fallon was born on June 16, 1931, in San Francisco, California, to Mark Fallon and Cecile Fallon (Cahill). His father's family were Irish-American Catholics; his mother's family were French-speaking Irish Catholics from Montreal, Canada. Both families were Democrats, which Joel's wife Carolyn said satisfied the unofficial requirement that you needed to be both Catholic and Democratic to live in San Francisco in those days.

The first grandchild of both families, Joel grew up with strong family support and nurturing from his three unmarried uncles and both sets of grandparents. He attended Catholic schools, including St. Ignatius. Carolyn said he hated it and that it "must have been dreadful for his family because they forced him to go there."

Joel was read to early and often as a child, which developed his love for literature. He learned French from his family and at school, developing an affinity for languages early on. One of his uncles sailed in and out of the San Francisco Yacht Club, so Joel was taught to sail. He swam with the Olympic Club and traveled the city in an era when a first-grader could safely take the streetcar alone. His was a happy, inclusive boyhood growing up in the Richmond District of San Francisco.

His poems about childhood reflect that experience.

Digging to China

I can't recall how we got the idea.
It seemed so reasonable. After all
we were five and had the tools.
Why not dig to China?
Surely we'd be there in time for lunch.

Somehow your mom's vegetable garden
was destroyed and you got a lump on your forehead
where the shovel handle
thumped you. Crying was optional.
You chose not to.

When the hole was knee deep we were
out of breath and
our hands were blistered.
We paused often to listen
for Chinese voices.

We had to pee but weren't ready
to abandon the job and go into your house.
A nosy neighbor telephoned your mother.
She erupted into the backyard, whooping
and screaming that I was a nasty boy.

To Kill a Snake

Swim suited, slim shanked,
we stalk a snake that
had presumed to startle us that
high Sierra afternoon
to whir-r-r urgently.
"Don't tread on me."

The civil warning is disregarded
because, I think, at twelve,
we are not civilized.

A mongoose does not debate
or weigh the merits as it sets out
to kill a snake. Nor do we.
The snake must die because it is a snake.
We have to kill the snake because we are twelve.

Galvanized, I find a branch and,
after posturing, pin the snake
to the killing ground.
My pal raises a sharp stone
and strikes and strikes again.

Not satisfied, we skin the snake,
soak the skin and salt it, and set it
to dry in the high Sierra sunlight.

Am I more civilized today?

The Mean Man

We groaned when our scruffy ball
arced over the cyclone fence
into the mean man's yard.

Somebody would have to ring
his bell and ask the mean man
for the ball. Or else the morning
would be ruined.

Wilson said he wouldn't go.
And Miller said
he wouldn't either.
So I said I'd try.

I rang the bell
and waited,
half hoping
that he wasn't home.

The pajama'd mean man,
unshaven, red eyed,
opened the door, and
looked at me.

His face was crumpled.
He said he'd open the gate and
that I could get the ball

And that I should stay
the hell away from his house.
I found the ball, yelled thanks, and ran out.

There are many mean men
and you don't always
get your ball back.

Paperboy

Fog before dawn. Streetlights flick off. Dark and damp.

The paperboy, an independent businessman at age thirteen,
knows all of the excuses —
and he expects to hear them.
Yet, off he strides with a springing step and a monstrous
heavy canvas bag striking him — chest and back.

Walking, folding, throwing.

He enters an unlocked apartment building and rides the
elevator to the twelfth floor.
Bag jammed into the door — he delivers six papers —
descends and stops at other floors.

On the sidewalk the bag is lighter. In the east a glow,
not sun but neon.
A streetcar thunders by.

Walking, folding, throwing over railings, up the stairs, onto
porches and balconies — push this one through
the mail slot.

He confirms the count — glad to have one extra,
and hurries, humming as he throws again and again.
Then — at a corner he listens for a streetcar
knowing he can exchange the extra for a free ride
to within a block of his home.

Spitfire – San Francisco

We built a Spitfire Mark V on a card table
in the dining room of a one bedroom apartment
above a soda fountain on the corner of 19th Avenue and
California Street. Louis lived there. I lived in the next block.

He owned the Spitfire and was chief of construction.
I was his assistant, in charge of scrounging razor blades
and pins. The Spitfire came in a cardboard box with sheets
of balsa wood, tissue paper, decals, and a large paper plan.

To assemble the Spitfire, we cut out precisely curved frames,
stamped on balsa wood, sliced strips of balsa wood
stringers, set the frames on stations and glued the slender
stringers to them.

As the Spitfire took form it grew more beautiful. We didn't
care that it lacked a Merlin Engine and fuel tanks and
Hispano twenty millimeter guns.
Instead, we focued on getting the wings' six-degree
dihedral just right.

Sighting along the stringers' sweet curves
we lovingly sanded high spots to make sure its
paper skin would lie properly on its wooden bones.
We doped the paper to shrink and tighten it and
after the paint and decals it looked — operational.

Finally, in cool San Francisco twilight, we climbed to Louis'
roof, lit it afire and launched it out over California Street.
The Spitfire soared gloriously for four blazing seconds
then crashed onto the asphalt by the streetcar tracks.

Best Day, Worst Day

The best day and the worst day
when I launched the first boat I ever built
in the surf
at China Beach.

I was fourteen,
fearless
and more than a little
stupid.

The best day,
a bright sunshiny day,
sparkling water, and
a fresh breeze.

The worst day,
when, fifty yards off shore,
she took on water and
sank in three fathoms.

Some parts of her may still be there,
with chunks of my heart,
hazards
to navigation.

Sex Education

Cliff House overlooks
Seal Rocks which glowed
in the Camera Obscura.

Cliff House was a magnet to me.
Not the fancy restaurant, but the lower stories
where Automata creaked and whirled,
and a ricky ticky piano played,
and a stand sold tacky souvenirs.

Cliff House had a book machine.
Put in a coin, push a button, and out
popped a book. A Little Blue Book
Edited by E. Haldeman-Julius.

Titles included:
Chemistry For Beginners,
What is a Hermaphrodite?
Hints on Public Speaking,
Studies in Psychosexuality and
Oddities of Sexual Behavior.

At twelve I had no interest in
chemistry or public speaking.
I was fascinated by the sexy titles.

Yet, by the time I arrived
every Saturday morning, the sexy
titles had all been sold.

Accordingly, I bought Book
number 613 *Ancient Philosophers,*
number 179 *Gems From Emerson,*
and 649 *The Egypt of Yesterday.*

I read these Little Blue Books
on the streetcar going home.
E. Haldeman-Julius educated me
by default. My parents and teachers
were impressed but I felt I remained,
well – sexually untutored.

Lilac Vegetal

My father sloshes Lilac Vegetal onto
rough palms and pats just-now shaven cheeks.
"Ahhhh," he sighs, as it stings his face.
The lush lilac scent fills the steamy bathroom.
He smiles at me and winks, towels mist from the mirror,
and asks if I'm ready for school.

I still recall the smells of childhood; of camphorated oil
rubbed on my chest when I was ten and had a cold; and
fragrances of cod liver oil and Sen Sen.
Graham crackers, seaweed, corned beef and cabbage; and
Coleman's dry mustard, mixed with beer. Can you smell
warm sourdough bread, the garlic and bleu cheese?

Leafy, dog-hair smell — our spaniel, back from
playing in the park; the struck match and languorous
smoke from dad's just-lit cigar. The smell of oily toolbox
in the Plymouth. The ice truck's fresh, cold, wet-wood smell.
And odors of hot dogs and cotton candy at
Playland at the Beach.

Smells of my childhood recall happy times
of trust, of safety and of privilege.
I think that sadder times must be remembered by
smells from childhoods spent in Hanoi,
or Srebrenica,
or Baghdad.

Young Man at Sea

In his junior year in high school, his father, "who knew everyone in town," helped Joel to enroll in the Longshoremen's Union. Joel trained and qualified as a common seaman. His summer job that year, 1948, at the age of 17, was to ship out as a merchant seaman sailing to China and the Philippines.

This began his love of the sea.

There wasn't much to do aboard the ship after his duty shifts so he spent time watching the ship's track across the Pacific Ocean. Joel consumed the ship's small library, reading with abandon. He especially enjoyed the large volume of English language poetry. This developed into a lifetime interest in reading the works of past and present poets, famous and infamous. It also sparked an interest in writing his own poetry to capture and record his life experiences.

The following poems are drawn from that summer at sea.

Bonus

We slipped
through the Golden Gate
one August morning
in 1948.
The harbor was full
of activity.

That afternoon
I signed off,
drew my pay,
settled accounts and
paid my union dues.
There was extra money
I hadn't counted on.

Gus said,
"Bonus for sailing
in mined waters."
I laughed out loud.
I was seventeen —
and immortal.

Lifeboat

Part of the Andrew Furuseth School of Seamanship
was a dingy loft on the Embarcadero. The other part was
San Francisco Bay. It linked us to the whole universe of water.
Red, our instructor, had many lessons to teach us before our
initiation into the Sailor's Union of the Pacific.
.
Time came to begin learning to handle a lifeboat.
We boarded with anticipation, eight young men and Red –
our teacher, mentor, bosun, coxswain – all rolled into one.

"All of you, hands off the gunnels."
Many didn't understand him.
"If this boat was a teacup, you'd put yer mouth
here on the gunnel to drink." He slapped an enormous
callused hand on the gunnel farthest from the pier.

As a good teacher's luck had it, the whaleboat caught some
small surge and gnashed its gunnel agonizingly against a
piling. His eyes twinkled. "That's why ya keep hands off the gunnels.
They'll pinch yer fingers clean off."

That morning we learned to raise, and lower, and feather
and ship and pull on the long heavy oars. He promised to buy
a new oar for anybody who broke one pulling on it. We raised
blisters and began to see the value and importance of working
together as a crew.

Red was a stickler for safety. It wasn't that he loved us –
although perhaps in a way he did. "Things are tough enough
without a body getting hurt. Take care of yerself so you'll not
be a burden to yer shipmates."

Later, as we rowed back to the pier, we saw ourselves
and each other differently.
And we kept our hands off the gunnels.

Flying Fish

Stand in the forepeak,
scan the sea ahead and
feel the ship's great heartbeat,
making speed for Manila.

Watch the schools of flying fish
pursued by swift indigo shades.
Frantic tails lash the sea.

Eager wings beat the foam.
With magnificent power of will
they fly a hundred yards or more.

Unless great hungry sea birds rip
into the formation
to catch unwary flyers.

Then, they fall back into the sea.
They churn and leap again, flying
into the salty sunkissed afternoon.

Outrunning coursing albacore
and wily blues, evading death squadrons,
they swim and leap and fly.

Perhaps at dusk, out on the
broad ocean reach, they can
take a breather, hoard their strength
and plot tomorrow's course.

Infinite Shades of Blue

We left at dusk,
our ship — a speartip
trailing a luminous shaft
arching westward.

> At dawn, far offshore,
> farther than I'd been before,
> the light revealed one of the sea's
> infinite shades of blue.

I was so drenched in blue
that years later I'm still not dry.
It's not simple to describe that blue,
not simple, but I'll try.

> Remember the tranquil blue
> of the blond girl's eyes?
> How I envied
> her eyelids.

The splash of dark blue forms
hurtling behind the flying fish
and — to the north the ominous
slate blue of an approaching squall.

> Or the faint blue veins
> pulsing beneath her skin,
> there — where she
> wasn't tan.

And the dancing blue flame
from the cutting torches
where they were
breaking up a vessel.

> Infinite shades of blue
> defy description. But this is clear —
> each shade of blue, in memory,
> I still hold dear.

Shanghai, '48

Four days in port
and Shanghai is insane.
Communists surround the city.
The banks have failed and we wade
ankle-deep in useless banknotes.

My eighteenth birthday and I buy
a scarf. All I can afford after gambling
my pay before we docked.
Play ping-pong with a Russian sailor.

Nationalists fleeing
to Formosa, but the beer remains —
excellent and cheap.

Back to my ship with scarf,
the taste of beer and a smile after
beating the Russian
two out of three.

Manila Bay

The pilot was aboard by seven.
Then, slowly we approached Manila.
Mid summer. A hot haze
hung over the oily bay.

Masts and kingposts stood dimly, desolately
in the blue haze
marking wrecks bombed, torpedoed or scuttled,
leaking fuel and memories.

Small brown men began unloading.
After a time I went ashore to take in the sights
and sounds.

Families in the concrete caves
of Rizal Stadium. Mules pulling carriages.
Loose fitting shirts concealing automatics.

Makeshift soft drink stands — no ice.
Vegetables, fruit, beer.
Music blaring from a speaker
on a wooden pole.

Women speaking soft sounds of Tagalog.
A child carrying another child.
Shirtless man, yelling
drunk outside a *panciteria*.
Pervasive smell of urine on concrete.

I walked for hours before returning to the ship,
to think of the wonders I had seen, and the wonders
I still had before me.

Persistent Illusion

Einstein, in a letter to a friend, wrote,
"Time is an illusion, but it is an amazingly
persistent illusion."
A persistent illusion?
Perhaps.

On the piano roll of time
I hear again the music of my youth,
music I heard at sea
on a ship that now sails only
in memory.

We had a record player on the ship
and two records.
We played those records
again and again.
Music and voyage blended and fused.

Half a century later the music plays
and I'm seventeen again in the North Pacific.
The engine throbs
and there's work to do
and all is well.

Jumping Ship

Before the voyage
you signed ship's articles
acknowledging the master's power
and officers' and bosun's too.

Underway with shipmates
you stand watch, chip, paint
and do the other chores
needed for the ship's well being,
and your own.

But now you've got the wind up and
you think of jumping ship.
Was that your idea from the onset
even before embarking? To quit?

You'll never catch another ship.
They've got your "Z" number.
Your berth will go to a man
the master can trust — who won't let
his shipmates down.

Ashore with a change of clothes,
a razor and some cash. Passport, visa? No.
Melt into the mass of congenial folks
in Yokohama, Valparaiso, Manila — right?
So how good is your Japanese, Portuguese, Tagalog?

When cash is gone who'll help or hire you?
Think again. Plan your life and live your plan.
Jumping ship's
not such a good idea.

The Soldier

*Beneath the chopper
sunlight glints from stained glass shards.
Rice paddies at noon.*

Haiku, Joel Fallon

The summer of 1948 was also the year China fell to the forces of Mao Zedong and his communist armies. In his several ports of call, Joel witnessed the turmoil of that time, with province after province falling to the "Red Menace." In at least one port he witnessed the bodies of the vanquished floating down the rivers from the interior to the sea.

Most young American men coming of age during the forties and World II embraced the meaning of patriotism and our duty to serve our country. We assumed military service was an honor and that we owed that duty to our nation. With his love for the sea, Joel applied to the California Maritime Academy in Vallejo. Although he passed the entrance exams with flying colors, he couldn't pass the physical due to having contracted amoebic dysentery in China during his Pacific cruise.

Six months after graduating from high school, Joel changed course by enlisting in the Air Force, where he again aced the entrance exams. After basic training, the Air Force sent him to the military language school in Monterey to learn to speak, read, and interpret the Russian language. His assignment was to listen to intercepted Russian communications for military intelligence.

But he was recently married and the $80 per month enlisted military pay didn't go very far. When he discovered that with his language skills he could become an officer in the Army, he applied for Army Officer Candidates School (OCS) in Fort Benning, Georgia. Upon graduation, he was promoted to the rank of Second Lieutenant and sent back to the Monterey Language School to learn Mandarin Chinese. Over his 21 years of military service, he rose from the entry level rank of an enlisted Airman Basic to become an Army Lieutenant Colonel.

He served all over the world, often leaving his family behind for months at a time. Where possible, they joined him in his postings in Germany, Japan, and for 5 years in the Philippines. While there, he completed a college degree in International Relations at the University of the Philippines. One of his last duties was a year-long posting as regimental commanding officer at a Russian listening post on Shemya Island at the end of Alaska's Aleutian Islands within sight of the Russian mainland. The only civilians on the island were Army employees supporting the military, so again his family was left behind in service to his country.

The poems in this short section reflect upon and commemorate that service.

Care and Cleaning

In barracks for Care and Cleaning of Equipment –
shine boots, tighten bunks, sew on patches, clean web gear.
Prepare for inspection.

Recruits who sign up for Korea
hear old soldiers from other outfits,
other times.

How to walk a post, pitch a tent,
clean weapons, keep warm in the field,
stay alive.

Down centuries wisdom passes – old to young.
Wrap your leggings, care for pack animals,
handle a sucking chest wound.

In Gaul, Roman veterans
of skirmishes with the Alemanni
supervise care and cleaning of equipment.

Sharpen sword and pilum.
Test leather harnesses and shields.
Stand fast. Do your duty. Stay alive.

Coach and Pupil

Privates first class, corporals, and
buck sergeants lie, two by two,
on ponchos at the range.
Coach and pupil — rifle marksmanship,
increasing some other bastard's chance to die.

Coaches observe, advise, encourage;
dole out a round, stress sight picture.
Pupils listen, take up slack, call their shot,
note hits, adjust sights and receive
another round. Again, again.

At morning break a safety check
and top off canteens with canvas-flavor water
from the Lister bag. Roll a smoke,
chew some REDMAN.

The pit detail comes to the firing line
to become coach and pupil.
We field strip our butts and move,
route step, to the pits to pull, mark and paste.

At mid-day, the cooks arrive to feed us.

Late afternoon, march back to the company area,
clean weapons, prepare for flag detail.

All time bespoken, all hands employed,
taxpayers get their money's worth.

Artillery Training, a Day Well Spent

First light, in the field, mess kit breakfast
Smell of canvas. Eggs, canteen cup of coffee.
Battery on line, trails spread, dug in.
Aiming stakes out, sights mounted, bubbles level.

Cannoneers' hop, slow dance training, again and again.
Rotate, learn all jobs. Simulate fire missions.
Now learn about trajectories, plunging fire, creeping fire,
Barrages, fire plans. Maintain tubes, pack bearings.

Again, the chow line. Tube steak, beans and golden peaches
in camouflage green cans, open with your P-38. Then
Hump ammo. Build rounds to order under sergeant's eye.
Powder bags in casings – topped with High Explosive Anti-Tank.

Ram round home. Slam breech shut.
Azimuth, elevation right, tug lanyard.
Gun roars and bucks – the round's away, taste brass?
Open block, extract casing. Again, again, again.

At dusk, soft rain falls, unheard by sound-shocked ears.
Fire last missions. Then, March Order.
Close trails, wrestle lunettes to pintles.
Main body heads for the barn.

A small detail polices the area,
And burns unused powder in a pit.
Nobody hurt, lessons learned.
Teams worked hard, a day well spent.

Anti-Tank Team

It takes a special kind of cojones
to stand up to a tank;
a special kind of "what the hell"
and the ability to penetrate thick armor
with your thought —
to see the driver's flesh and blood,
to feel the gunner's pulse beating in his helmet.
Try hard and you can smell their breath
and tell what they ate for lunch.

Set aside the terrifying size and
mighty bulk of the tank.
Don't get hypnotized by its
horrible noise and how it
gobbles up landscape.

Focus on the driver and the gunner.
If you use what you have,
and use it well, they won't eat lunch again.
Ever.

On the Cable Line Road

We marched on the Cable Line Road,
barely a road at all, just
a faint track connecting two points,
two worlds, Camp Stotsenburg and
Camp O'Donnell.

Strange to say those words after fifty years.
Stotsenburg an Army Post, home of the 26th Cav,
swallowed up by Clark Air Base
and Camp O'Donnell, the POW camp where
survivors of the Bataan march were kept
less hospitably than animals in a zoo.

They too had marched on the Cable Line Road.
And when they were tired and too sick
to march they were bayoneted and
fell to the side of the Cable Line Road.

The Japanese surrendered years before
but as we marched we remembered.
Moving silently, at route step, we stopped
every hour or so to smoke and sip
from our canteens.

We remembered and measured ourselves
against the old soldiers
who had marched here,
between worlds,
on the Cable Line Road.

Coming Home

Finished – ten years of war
for pillage, for honor, and to reclaim
sluttish Helen, kidnapped
by the Prince of Troy.

They outfoxed the Trojans and sacked their city.
Stabbing, hacking, slashing.
They raped the women, and defiled the corpses.
Then – they set sail for home.

Having dealt death by sword, by bayonet,
by rifle, by napalm, can warriors really come home
or will they always be assaulted by the noise,
the bodies and the smell of the dead?

Night is dark and the road is long.
What is left of the old life?
How much has changed? Are the children grown?
Did wives yield to lusty suitors?

A long steep road coming home
from Troy, from Guadalcanal,
from My Lai and Waziristan
to happy ever after.

Slender Colonel

He remained slender after it was over. The forced march,
years ago in the heat, and the death of
fellow soldiers as they fell out along the way,
profoundly changed him.

Even his sense of humor had been changed.
He found things humorous that you and I wouldn't.

Returning to Clark was, for him, like coming home.
Because it had happened here;
or more precisely, at Stotsenberg,
adjacent to Clark Field.

When the Japanese approached, a few officers and men had
faded into the ravines and tall clumps of bamboo, hoping to
hook up with the negritos. Most had stayed, although they
knew they were too lightly armed to make much difference.

They did their jobs right up to the end, maintaining communications
from Stotsenberg, up the Cable Line Road to the transmitter site at
Camp O'Donnell. Then, the Japanese arrived.

Now, years later, after cataclysmic events, the death march, prison,
it was peacetime and he was back again
in the Philippines,
commanding a battalion.

In the delicious warm evenings he played bridge with his wife
and his officers and their wives. Wearing an aloha shirt,
he served gin and tonics and smiled
at things we didn't understand.

Explosive Ordnance

You've seen the movie
a fiendishly clever time bomb is going to explode — soon.
An expert huddles over the bomb trying to decide how to disarm it.
Tension mounts. A digital clock counts down the seconds.

The expert makes a desperate choice
and at the last possible instant disarms the bomb —
keeping New York or Chicago or Denver from being vaporized
and winds up with the unbelievably beautiful wisecracking babe.

There are Explosive Ordnance Demolition experts.
They do disarm dangerous objects like bombs and land mines.
Sometimes they lose their lives — then, their believably
ordinary wives search for the insurance policy.

In Korea

In Korea,
there was a song we sang
during the war and it was
The Band Played China Night.
Actually, a Japanese song
written to commemorate
the Japanese adventures in Manchuria.
But it was updated and we sang it in Korea,
The Band Played China Night.
What a night in China —
What a night in China!

Stern soldiers in quilted coats strained southward.
In Japan, the cooks and clerks drew rifles
and kissed the girls goodbye and
The Band Played China Night.
Harbor lights, deep purple night —
the quilted soldiers erupted south
and the line bent and broke,
and the fertile land was washed in blood, and
The Band Played China Night.
What a night in China —
What a night in China!

We fought north and bled again
and restored the line
and fresh troops came and
The Band Played China Night.
What a night in China,
a Dream Night.

Penicillin

Within a week of shipping out to Korea in the 1950s,
I came down with a bad sore throat. A doctor at Fort Ord
examined me and said, "Two hundred thousand units of Penicillin."
That was good information to have. After the shot I was fine within hours.

Six months later, in Korea - another horrible sore throat.
I went to a Mobile Army Surgical Hospital (MASH) and told the doctor
(a major) I wanted two hundred thousand units of penicillin.
Eying my Infantry insignia, he asked, "Are you a doctor?"
"No sir," I replied.

"Well, lieutenant, I figure you're trying to get rid of a dose of clap.
Get your ass outta here!"

I left and drove to another MASH on the outskirts of town, thinking
about the lesson I had just been given. At the second MASH, I said,
"Doctor, I've got a terrible sore throat. Please look at it." Peering down
my throat he said, "H-m-m, two hundred thousand units of penicillin."
After that shot I was fine within hours.

Moral: Don't break anybody else's rice bowl. Stick to what you know.

Isn't that what Columbus and the Wright brothers did?

Romel's Buried Treasure

During the cold war,
as we waited
for the Soviets to thrust
into the Fulda Gap.
Romel's buried treasure
from World War II
was found in North Africa.

Eight railcars of hooch —
gin, scotch, nasty tasting bourbon
and cognac like the tears of angels.
Our heroic morale officer
outdid himself re-importing it
to West Germany, where it sold quickly
in the CLASS VI store.

Drinking history late one night
in my quarters in Frankfurt,
I thought of John, my mom's
kid brother shot down near Rabat
and sold to the German Army by
the friendly Arabs.

Romel's treasure, guarded by
generations of scorpions, was found
close to where his plane had augered in.
Now, I was drinking treasured cognac
close to the Stalagluft
where John, a POW, sat out the war.

He was never a drinker himself.
When he came home after VE Day
he stuck with RC Cola.
Nonetheless, I drank to John and to
the treasure's guardian scorpions.

Snapshots of Life

Mrs. Butterworth

Waffles, juice and coffee
with the sweetest gal on earth –
do you think her husband knows
just how sweet she is?

When a poet merely observes and, like an artist, sketches what he sees, the result is a "snapshot" of his world. If it makes a statement, instructs, brings a smile or a tear, we all get a bonus.

My Town

My town is a river town at the edge of land,
where Sierra water, tired from working in rice fields,
meets the Pacific — then swirls off
in current, fog and cloud.

My town's front yard is three miles wide
with fishing boats and deep draft tankers.
Seals play here, barking and calling at night,
each to each. That sound sweetens the silence.

News of the gold strike spread from here to the world.
In my town pony express riders swapped horses,
and Jack London drank here deep and often.

The arsenal of my river town supplied rifles
and cannon for skirmishes along the Snake
and Feather rivers and Guadalcanal,
and Yong Dong Po, and Khe Sanh.

In its time, an Army town,
a ship-building town with whores and hooligans,
a town of rough edges,
not yet all smoothed down.

My river town is quieter now
and almost all the silvery shopping carts
return to nest outside the grocery stores
at night — when streetlights
drip buttery pools onto
the tilty sidewalks.

I Walked Again on the Beach Today

I walked again on the beach today
early, before the sun had chased away
the fog.

I walked in morning's misty memory
back through time to where, a child, I'd walked
before

and gulls strode with me on the sand
and cried and cried sad cries
again.

In bygone days there in the surf
great broken timbers darkly rolled
restless

there in the creamy surf like
old men turning fitfully
in bed.

Now on the beach mighty timbers
with rusting ring bolts are seen but
rarely.

Instead, man's immortal debris
litters sand and shore. Cry now — sad cries
indeed.

Under These Roofs

From the long downgrade there's a
sweep of roofs in the morning haze;
tar and gravel, galvanized,
composition, metal and shake.

And under these roofs: attics of musty trunks,
boxed vinyl records,
dressmakers' dummies,
old Monopoly sets.

And under these roofs: people
on honeymoon, coupling, uncoupling;
families with infants,
kids watching cartoons
in the family room.

Toast pops from toasters
and the smell of coffee.
Bacon snaps in the pan,
orange juice being unconcentrated.

And in the offices and schools
lights come on and janitors change
into overalls
and high school principals
drink a shot of vodka.

Laundromat

Crowded, warm and humid.
Smells of soap powder
and bleach.

The Filipina sits watching the
clothes kaleidoscope in the dryer
as her children busy themselves –
all except Angela.

Angela, about five, is cranky and needs a nap.
A boy and two older girls fold and stack,
fold and stack.

The mother seems worried as Angela
sits with her underwear
exposed.

I avert my eyes and mother
relaxes a notch or two.
The dryer stops.

Mom speaks rapid Tagalog.
The children smile and answer
in English.

They unload the clothes,
fold them quickly
and fill plastic baskets.

Gathering baskets of clean clothes
and Angela, they drive off
in a late model sedan.

The Green Street Marching Band

Faint at first, the heartbeat of their drum.
Traffic's slowing as they come.
Now, marking time at Portsmouth Square,
unmindful of the tourists' stare,
the drummer beats a 'tak-tak-tak.'

Ah, striding out they sound so grand,
the jaunty Green Street Marching Band.
In Chinatown we hold our breath
knowing music marks the death
of a respected man.

"Oh when the saints come marching in ..."
Sunlight bounces from their brass.
"When the saints come marching in ..."
Storefront windows rattle.
"Regard the time and fly from evil."

Sights and sounds of death and life,
hanging ducks, live crabs and fish in tubs,
vegetables in fine array and flags and signs and
church and temple and smells of sweat,
and sweet and sour.

They knit it all together
and roll it in their hand
and strut into eternity —
the Green Street Marching Band.

The Eucalyptus

Before I came, they were here already,
the eucalyptus.
"From Australia," they said,
as if to convey in that brief phrase
the whole story of their journey.

No matter, they're here now,
standing in stately columns
beside the roads,
with slats of golden light
streaming between.
They soften the breeze
and please the eye.

Tall graceful warriors,
with long spears of cinnamon bark,
they squint into the sun,
swaying to ancient rhythms,
whispering private words.

I think Australia
must smell like home.

Naked Ladies on the Russian River*

I saw them at Sebastapol,
a sorority of naked ladies
all cat's-tongue pink
and bending down.

From Jenner to Monte Rio, legions
of Loreleis flaunting their beauty
beckoning drivers
on the River Road.

Blushing, buck-ass naked ladies
peeking through iron fences
in Guerneville, whispering to oleander
smiling shyly.

*(Belladonna Lily, Amaryllis: plants of the genus
Amaryllis are known as...naked lady)*

River Child

I dreamt a river child,
a sad dream just before dawn.
I watched in the darkness as the land became shiny,
shiny and strange — there were no eucalyptus trees
but the oaks were thick. And I watched figures moving
in the oak groves, gathering acorns, and I saw deer
and, on the river, more ducks and pelicans
than I had ever seen.

There was a child by the river
and as the sun rose higher, I watched the river child.
She was slender and her dark hair was braided.
She wore strange, graceful clothes,
and was gathering something, clams perhaps, from the shore
and placing them into a basket.
She moved slowly toward a clump of reeds,
stooping and putting things into the basket
until she was lost to my sight.

When I woke the eucalyptus trees were back and
the oaks seemed stunted. The groves were empty
and the deer and ducks and pelicans were gone.
So was the river child.

And I realized I loved her.

The Cut-Away Man

A magazine beckons travelers to Greece,
great values now in low season.
Squeezed on one page is
a photo of a Greek column,
tightly cropped — hardly an inch of air
between it and the printed words.
A layout decision — or is there something
I'm not meant to see?

The smiling girl in the photo album
is much older now.
One side of her picture
has been cut away.
Was she happy? What went wrong?
Does she think I can't see the fingers
of the hand on her hip — the hand of
the cut-away man?

It seems that there must always be
things I may not know —
how warm it was
that day in Greece
and how the Ouzo clouded in the glass.
The songs they sang,
the smiling girl and the cut away man.

Mister Baraban Forgives God

God doesn't mess with Mister Baraban much.
His parents and beloved wife, Vera, died long ago.
He had prayed for Vera's life but God had other plans.
Baraban loves God but can't forgive him.

Baraban did not forgive God for His shabby treatment
of Adam and Eve either. I mean, just one little slip …?
And Job too. Why had God been so unforgivably harsh?

Baraban swears in Russian like his father did.
He says, "Devil take you!" and means it.
For sneezes Baraban says, "God bless you."
He means that too.

Older now, Baraban is starting to mellow.
He still swears and asks for blessings but he has begun
to forgive God for his parents and for Vera,
and for his own increasing fragility.

Apples and Worms

An apple without a worm
is to enjoy.
An apple with a worm
is less enjoyable.
An apple with half a worm
is enjoyment interrupted.

Life would be sad
without apples.
Life would be unthinkable
without worms.

Mountain Woman

In the doctor's waiting room,
parchment pale,
storm bird amidst
sandpipers.

She knows candles, kerosene,
fire on the hearth;
and is content, also —
with darkness.

Maker of quilts, poultices,
scuppernong wine.
Setter of bones. Baker of bread.
Singer of hymns.

At home with wood smoke,
dulcimer, and guitar.
In adversity —
steadfast.

She nods at
what the doctors say —
then, gets well anyway.
She always has.

Mercy of October

She set a splendid table.
He mixed a mean martini.
Slender, tan and quick to smile,
members of our church and rotary.

The golden couple left last fall —
driving eastward in brisk morning.
Their upscale house in escrow,
neighbors wished them *bon voyage*.

A well-deserved promotion,
in his company back east.
They drove away and left two cats
to the mercy of October.

Old Images

How cumbersome the camera was,
the tripod too and box of plates.
The fuss to get the light just so,
to make the whole thing straight and true
was almost more than they could stand.

Important too that everyone
be still, not thrash or mill about.
Regardless, trees moved in the wind
and water flowed and smoke
wafted where it would.

But it was worth the fuss because
it froze the women – dark dresses,
with their shoe tips peeking out and
mustached men in unpressed suits,
with vested bellies fobbed and chained.

All so unhurried, simple and
everybody seemed to know that
you and I would study them and
so they wore their Sunday faces.
Strong and plain – sure and beautiful.

Detective Story

The Stuttgart Bahnhof was busy. Not crowded,
but busy. I checked the station's clock, consulted
the schedule and found the correct rail car.

Warm compartment, jacket hung and heavy bag
wrestled onto overhead rack, I settled back into
the plush, second-class seat and lit a cigarette.
We all smoked in those days.

On the platform people bustled buying newspapers,
shaking hands and hugging.

We'd be on our way in eleven minutes.
Then, three hours to Munich, give or take.
Home in time for dinner. I opened a detective story,
Nicholas Freeling.

I turned a page or two then glanced out the window to see
another train ease into the station on the adjacent track.
Destination — Paris.
They might be home for dinner too.

A dark haired woman in the other car stood
gazing out the window. She was holding a book.
Its cover — the same as mine. She looked at me.
I raised my book. We both smiled as my train
left the station.

What is it about Milwaukee, Wisconsin?

What is it about Milwaukee, Wisconsin?
And why do we add the gratuitous word "Wisconsin"?
Is there a Milwaukee in Wyoming or
North Carolina?

In the theater of my skull
the name Tombstone starts the
projector.
I see a small town, circa 1870 or so,
cowboys, open range, a picturesque cemetery.

Next, I see Tokyo — early morning smoke from
thousands of charcoal fires and,
oh so rarely
in winter, distant Fuji levitating
like a tranquil Zen master.

But the name Milwaukee evokes no image.
And — adding Wisconsin doesn't help.
Perhaps one day Milwaukee will be so famous
a picture appears and people in Tombstone and Tokyo
won't feel compelled to add Wisconsin.

Walk on the Beach

Almost noon. Park on the Great Highway,
where the "B" streetcar used to come.
Lock our jackets and lunch in the trunk.
Walk down the concrete steps to the white sand.

Take off your Keds. Hang them around your neck
with knotted laces. Roll up your pant legs and walk
through the sand toward the sea.

Quickly, the sand is hot. But cautiously — broken glass,
where hyenas left their mark.

Ahead, the sea, with rollers having traveled thousands of
miles — to break on the beach again and again. A clean
sea-smell.

Speaking loudly now
so that we can hear over the thunder of the surf.
Let's walk north on the cool damp hard packed sand,
through the mist toward the Cliff House overlooking Seal Rocks.

Dogs chasing frisbees. Children laughing.
An old man sitting in a lawn chair — bare chested,
squinting toward China. Tide destroying sand castles.
The sea swiftly slides in over the glistening brown sand
shocking our feet with cold kisses.

Unseen creatures sigh blown bubbles in the sand as the
sea recedes. A tangle of kelp sloshes in the shallows
and a tiny cautious crab scuttles toward the foam.

Crying gulls ignore the body surfers. We watch a small
boy with a sandwich. He is famished. So am I.
Let's head back to the car for our lunch.

Marginalia

Sometimes I come across a book,
second hand of course, in which
a reader has jotted down his thoughts
on the margins of the page.

Those thoughts are better than free
because they make the book much cheaper
for the buyer —
me.

And there's the fun of crawling through
the air ducts of the reader's mind
to see how he contorts his face while jotting notes,
underscoring lines of text and adding punctuation marks.

Surely he must know the meaning of *rotund*,
banal and *moribund*.
But why put an exclamation point right here?
Did truth emerge all shimmering and clear?

If you, like I, enjoy a splash of marginalia
perhaps you've noted too
that most persistent practitioners of the art
set aside their pens before the middle of the book.

By page one oh five the reader finds someone to love,
or loses his dictionary, or maybe Athena's ancient owl
now perches in his study, munching mice —
defecating definitions.

Sweet Water, Sweet Life

We'd fish here sometimes,
Uncle Gene and I. Right here in these waters.
I lived in San Francisco then and I'd meet Gene
at his boat early, five or so. He'd squirt some ether
into the big diesel and we'd head out
into the cool morning.

We'd run past Richmond and Red Rock and under the bridge.
We'd troll starting at San Pablo Bay.
Sometimes we'd drop the hook off Port Costa
but more often stop and bottom fish just about here.

This was all sweet water then.
Not so much chemical runoff from up river.
We'd sort of laze around, set the rods in holders,
ease tension on our reels and have
sandwiches and coffee.

Most often we'd catch our limit of striped bass.
There was no risk in eating fish then.
This was sweet water, no chemicals to speak of.
We never gave a thought to mercury.

Nowadays there's not much fishing here.
Hell, a man would be a fool to eat fish from this water.
Ever wonder where it went —
the sweet water, the sweet life?

Opinion Pages

At the end of Joel's 21-year military service, he retired and took a job in the Bay Area building concrete boats. Who builds concrete boats? Joel did, and quite well too, becoming the area go-to guy as an expert in concrete boat building and design. After three years, due to an industrial accident that blew out his knee, he could no longer do that type of heavy physical labor.

Joel then returned to work as a civilian employee of the Defense Department where he could use his language skills. He was sent to Germany with his family. He spent most of the next twenty years there until retiring and moving to Benicia, California. During his time in Germany, he became locally and narrowly famous for playing the roles of Russian officers in Defense Department films used for the training of overseas servicemen.

As an Army officer and Defense Department civilian employee, it was not his job to comment on or criticize the politics or policies of his employer, the United States Government. That didn't mean he had no opinion — he just didn't publicly express it or write about it. Once retired, he could and did give voice, with a good will and a strong sense of right and wrong.

The following poems reveal his views and personal moral compass.

Dirty Diaper Lie

He told a lie.
It wasn't a little private
white lie
but a big brown
dirty diaper lie;
and the messy stain
spread
and stunk.

Sometimes little white lies
can be absorbed
into the fabric of life
but a big
brown
dirty diaper lie is almost
well —
PRESIDENTIAL.

A Man is There

Unmindful of the future,
the cattle stand stately
or lie in the shade
unhurried, serene —

untroubled by political
parties, freedom of the
press or the Second
Amendment.

They will be rounded up
driven up a ramp, then
crowded tightly into
an eighteen wheeler.

A four-hour drive —
anxiety at first, then
fear and panic
before stopping.

Each is coaxed roughly
through a chute leading
to a slippery concrete floor
with heavy metal grates.

A man is there
with an automated
sledge hammer. He applies
it to each animal.

Cloud Children

In the Andes, atop a mountain top
where the air is thin.
That's where they've slept for centuries,
the cloud children.
Slept with golden toys around them,
buried, frozen.

They were guilty.

Other cloud children of Auschwitz
and Srebrenica
they were guilty too.
And those of Nadjaf, Amritsar,
Nanking – Guilty. Guilty. Guilty.

Their crime was trusting parents, governors,
and uncles.

Guilty of weakness –
guilty of yielding to the power of grownups.

Cloud children guilty
of living in a world where power
trumps weakness,
where lies
topple truth.

Hush, cloud children.
Hush and drink
your Kool-Aid.

Conversion

They walk in twos,
clean cut, white shirts
and ties
striding briskly,
no smiles,
god smoldering through
their eyes,
souls burning brightly,
lusting for converts.

At home their families
hoard dimes and quarters.
They lust for converts too.
Next week the young men
leave for Damascus.

Perhaps their paths
may cross those of
two other boys — zealots with
incandescent souls
on their way to San Francisco
to destroy a bridge.

Recognizing a common fervor,
will they nod as they pass?

Do Pigs Win?

The California Zephyr originates in Emeryville
and goes to Chicago.
It arrives in Martinez an hour late.
The official word is "train congestion." Whatever that is.

We board and move north and eastward.
Instead of making up time we lose it, constantly.
Somewhere between Winnemucca and Elko
in the dark of the first night, more than two hours behind, we stop.

Most passengers are asleep as
the unofficial word wafts through the car,
"They're changing engineers." We remain stopped
for over forty minutes. Then lurch into the night.

At Green River we are four hours late.
Passengers are muttering to themselves.
Cell phones are reporting the status of the "train from hell."
Somebody says, "Mussolini made the trains run on time."

Instead of arriving in Denver at seven thirty the second evening
we will arrive at two the following morning.
Should some AMTRAK CEO be eviscerated
and made to watch the California Zephyr
run over his glistening intestines in the cool of the morning?

Well, no. It seems that AMTRAK doesn't own the rails.
Other companies own them. Their trains — hauling lumber and
pigs to Chicago have priority over AMTRAK passenger trains.
So, do pigs win over passengers — every time?
"No, not really, passengers have a round trip ticket!"

Mid-East Questions

In Gaza and Ramallah boys are throwing stones at tanks
and tanks are plowing through buildings.
Dark women in black outfits pull their hair,
squeeze eyes tight and wail.

Crowds carry coffins covered with flags
and brandish big photos of dead youngsters.
Wild-eyed men on dusty roads shake their fists,
pumped up with hate.

Why are there so many youngsters on the street
in the middle of the day?
Why aren't they in school?

It seems like a movie set and all the extras
have been rounded up for crowd scenes.
What do they do when they aren't
making this movie over and over?

Aren't there any factories where they can
make cars, or refrigerators, or harmonicas?
Can't they grow cotton or tobacco,
or lima beans?

Is hate the only industry?
Does only death bring pleasure?

Neighborhoods Are Not a Game

Neighborhoods are getting worse, I think.
Stores are boarded up and jobs are scarce
down on **Baltic Avenue**.

There's graffiti on the fence in **Saint James Place** where none
used to be, and regiments of ragged men finger coin slots
in trashed phone booths — on their way to nowhere.

Gangs roam **Vermont Avenue**.
We hear drive-by shootings every night.
Still —there's bills to pay and taxes too.

Free Parking? Not a Chance.
Cough up the dough for utilities and rent.
Pay up, or hit the road.

Cops patrol in twos, on **Ventnor Avenue**.
Sharp eyes skim for soft drink cans in vacant lots
in shards of dreams and broken glass. No deposit, no return.

Some fixer-uppers bloomed on **States Avenue**.
But now that neighborhood is sliding into the ghetto
downhill — all the way.

Marvin Gardens has fresh paint and shrubs,
but life is tougher than it seems and
the middle class has cardboard in their shoes.

Neighborhoods are not a game.
Tip-toe past **BOARDWALK**. Shudder. Hold your breath,
and hitch your belt up to pass **GO** — one more time.

Over the Wall

Years ago my work took me
to eastern Turkey — to Diyarbakir,
an ancient city drowsing
on a black stone plateau.

Faithfully each morning my cab driver waited
at the Mardin Gate to take me to work.
Each afternoon he waited for my pleasure —

to shop, to see the sights,
the mosques, museums, the summer home
of Kemal Pasha Ataturk.

One afternoon, having seen old coins, swords and daggers,
he drove me to the east wall where the land tumbles steep
to a valley and the Tigris River dashes into Iraq.

"Here we threw the Christians over the wall in
the years of my grandfather." He shut his eyes
fighting back a smile.

He opened his eyes and gazed at me with
candles burned inside his skull
shining through his eyes.

"You are a Christian?"
"Yes, I'm a Christian."
We regarded each other silently.

As he realized this Christian was not
going over the wall today
the candles flickered out.

We returned to the hotel.
The next morning
he was not waiting for me.

Questions About an Armless Boy

Does the boy on the table,
the boy without arms,
feel "liberated"?

Does he think
his life has been improved
by the regime change?

Will he be able to cast a ballot,
salute a flag?
Will he even want to?

Is a crime committed
in the name of democracy
still a crime?

Is there a special place in hell
for those who did
this obscene thing to him?

Who will judge? Who will pay?
Who will tie his shoes?
Who will feed him?

Unknowing, a curious nation considers
there must be other horizons, other
less bloody alphabets.

Tilman Riemenschneider's Fingers

His fingers lightly held wooden handles
of exquisitely sharp carving tools.
Apprentices studied his grip, his stance, his words
but studied mostly the gothic miracles
he carved in fine grained wood.

Riemenschneider's miracles endure.
The holy family, apostles, saints, sinners and soldiers
carved on altar screens and panels
have breathed lightly for five hundred years.

Their wooden faces smile sadly
and — in the fading light
wooden limbs twist in wooden clothing
and blood and tears
flow from them.

Gazing at his artistry
we wonder how much more
Riemenschneider could have done.
What other beauty
might have been revealed,
had not some vengeful princeling
ordered his fingers to be broken?

Throw Out the Back Seat

World War Two movie, set in Nazi-occupied Holland —
someone is betraying the gallant resistance fighters to the Nazis.
Is it Clark Gable or Lana Turner or is it
Victor Mature? See for yourself.

Watch the Nazi motorcycle troops chase valiant
resistance fighters in their ancient Citroen sedan.
They speed crazily along a rutted dirt road by a canal.
Lugers (what else?) are waved and fired.

The car swerves, steadies and dashes on.
Pursuing Nazi motorcycles whine and churn.
"They're gaining, they're gaining. Oh God, what'll we do?"

They rip out the back seat of the old Citroen and heave it
out the window of the speeding car. The motorcycle troopers
swerve frantically to avoid the bouncing car seat. They lose
control and flip, ass over teakettle, into the canal.

We chuckle as Nazis shake their fists and the rejoicing
resistance fighters race away.

Modern car seats are difficult to remove but flinging them out
the back window is a splendid way to slow down pursuers
and make your getaway.

Watch modern politicians throw out the back seat when truth
is gaining on them. Watch the bad guys get away.

The Day He Died

The day he died in Iraq,
Barry Bonds punched another
out of the park —
and the crowd went wild.
And they pulled his broken body
from the Humvee.

The day he died in Iraq,
a new action movie broke
records at the box office —
and the crowd went wild.
And boys gouged out his eyes with dirty thumbnails.

The day he died in Iraq,
an eight-year-old girl was raped
in a San Francisco ghetto —
and the crowd didn't hear her screams.
And they doused him with gas
and set him ablaze.

The day he died in Iraq,
sweet smoke rose from a million barbecues —
and the crowd was diverted.
And when the meat had cooled
it was pulled from the bone.

Ziusudra, The Faraway (101)

Incised sharply on baked clay tablets
Are inventories, ledgers, and
business records of all sorts.
And, rarely, a curse to curl your hair.
That's what's found in most Sumerian digs.

But, exceptions do happen, and
when they do, a window opens
to a world more ancient than Homer's —
a world that somehow explains and
foreshadows ours, today.

Tablets say the gods decided to
wipe out man by a great flood;
but Enki the water god gave a warning to Ziusudra,
advising him to build a large boat.
Ziusudra did, and rode out the storm and was saved.

After the flood he sacrificed an ox and a sheep.
That pleased the gods and they granted Ziusudra
eternal life in a paradise, far away in Dilmun,
where the sun rises. The tablets call Ziusudra
"preserver of the name of man."

Newer tablets in Babylon give more details
than the Sumerian story. The captain, now called
Utnapishtim – "He who saw life,"
and his crew and cargo also survived.
And the captain was granted eternal life in the Faraway.

Genesis tells that God warned Noah a flood was coming,
and gave him instructions on building a boat.
When the heavens opened up Noah embarked with family and animals.
They survived. Noah gave thanks but was not granted eternal life,
he was cut down at age nine hundred and fifty.

Universe Rewound

He's fed up.
He's had enough.
He has stopped the universe
and pushed rewind.
And the universe begins to contract.

Clocks run backward, faster, faster.
Lincoln rises from an ancient grave.
Founding fathers are middle-aged,
now young adults, now children —
infants crawling back to dark wombs.

Columbus sails backwards to Spain.
The ceiling of the Sistine Chapel is
an uninspired field of egg-shell white.
The tower at Pisa straightens and is quickly unbuilt.
London has only wooden buildings.

Julius Caesar has breakfast then goes back to bed.
John the Baptist unwashes his face.
Noah is a child playing with a toy boat.
Adam is alone in the garden. Then he is gone
and the garden — and all the land is desolate.

Continents coalesce and are swallowed by the sea.
No day, no night — and in the gray twilight
stars start winking out.
The universe rushes in and
there is no yesterday.

The Humorist

Feed the Cat

We don't feed the cat.
We make food available.
The cat feeds himself.

Tuna

Agile, swift and pure
ferocious fighter — now just
chicken of the sea.

Hunter's Morning

My cat's mornings are all spent
sleeping in a shaft of light.
Perhaps he dreams of how he went
hunting in the dark of night.
He thinks his trophies pay the rent
and in a way he's right.

Joel always had a strong sense of humor. He honed his public speaking skill through Toastmasters Clubs and his acting roles in the military. Telling jokes was his forte, always with a smirk on his lips and a twinkle in his eye.

The following poems capture some of his delightful tongue-in-cheek humor.

High Crime or Misdemeanor

I made a mistake
because I didn't know what
a bidet was.
I shat in the mayor's wife's bidet.
I tried to hide the evidence but couldn't —
because the captain was yelling outside,
"Hurry up, lieutenant hurry up!"

We stayed with the mayor and his family last night.
Today we had business in town.
We returned in the early evening.
They waited dinner for us.
Conversation was strained.
I guess that was appropriate
since one of their guests had committed either
a high crime or misdemeanor.

I've tried unsuccessfully for years
to forget the incident.
I hope there is a new mayor now and that
his wife hasn't heard about the idiot
who shat in her bidet.

I Forget the Name of the Girl

I forget the name of the girl
I kissed in the rumble seat
that summer, long ago.
We had danced and she had
shown me some
sweet and graceful moves.

Now warm bodies close
under the stars
on a dark country road,
we warmed each other
and whispered low.
I kissed her hungry lips.

Kissing, we clung like mating
butterflies as the ancient roadster
hurtled through the night.
The kiss was interrupted
when the roadster crunched
over the railroad tracks.

She screamed and I cursed.
"You chipped my tooth!"
"I guess I did," I said.

21 Hayes to Shangri-La

Last month, late at night, a few poets and I boarded the 21 Hayes headed toward Market Street. It was just half full – night shift nurses from St Mary's and restaurant workers. After chatting with other poets I nodded sleepily. Soon I was jolted awake by a woman shouting, "We're going the wrong way." She was right. Looking through the window I saw that the bus was on Clement Street, almost to the Palace of the Legion of Honor.

The driver, a Latino when I got on, was now an Asian, wearing a leather flight helmet. The passengers were all different too – pimps and proctologists, pedophiles and podiatrists. One of them went forward to talk to the driver but was waved away when a wicked-looking automatic pistol was flourished.

We all settled back to await developments. The bus stopped briefly at the Palace of the Legion of Honor. A man got on. Nobody was allowed to exit. Then, unbelievably, the bus rose into the air and headed northeast on a great circle route to Asia. Hours later we descended, into a MacDonald's parking lot somewhere in Java. I say Java because the amber-colored, topless young ladies looked just like the perky Javanese women I had studied years ago in the National Geographic Magazine.

I rose to confront the driver. He was dead, slumped over the steering wheel, dribbling a theatrical trickle of blood onto his rumpled Muni jacket. A tall Asian man named Ch'ang escorted us all off the bus. He led me to the High Lama who he said wanted to speak with me. As I entered his candlelit chamber, the High Lama greeted me by name and asked me to stay here in Shangri-La – a place where you got what you wanted instead of what you deserved. I agreed to stay but only after settling some details at home – a wife, five kids, eleven grandchildren and a parking ticket in Walnut Creek.

We smiled at each other and I left. Outside I saw the amber-colored, bare chested, jiggly young Javanese ladies. Jiggle, jiggle – somebody was jiggling my arm. It was a poet saying, "Wake up, Joe. We're almost to Market Street."

Every now and then, late at night, I wait at the Palace of the Legion of Honor for a 21 Hayes on its way to Shangri-La.

A Man of Consequence

She got on the bus at Polk Street,
floated down the aisle
and sat next to me. Pleasant face.
Cotton candy hair
and improbable breasts —
smelling of bubble gum.

Clearly, I was of no consequence.

She would be unimpressed to know
I hold a black belt in FENG SHUI
and that I practice DIM SUM each day at dusk.
If I told her I am the president's
special envoy to the International
House of Pancakes she would
probably yawn — politely, of course.

When our thighs touched
I wondered if she heard my DNA
screaming that I wanted to get off
the bus with her at the next stop
and walk, arm in arm, under the neon,
in the cool of the evening — to her place.

In her queen-size bed, listening to Verdi,
we would soar, like mating eagles,
tumbling in the brilliant altostratus
of her sheets.

Later, she would comb her cotton candy hair
and we would walk, arm in arm, to the nearest
International House of Pancakes,
where, as the President's special envoy,
it would be clear to her that I *am*
a man of consequence.

Banned in Benicia

One morning blue-haired power walkers
saw them in the bookstore window,
two poetry books.

Angels on the cover of one book did not offend.
Angels rarely do.
But the cover of the other – holy cow –
a nekkid woman – on a bed!

The power walkers frowned.
They had been conceived by fully clothed
parents for whom intercourse
was a sacrament.

Clearly the nekkid woman on the bed
had been having fun and seemed prepared
to have it again and again.
Surely not sacramental.

The poetry book was removed
and word was circulated,
"Watch out for this guy,
he knows where babies really come from."

Another Part of the Forest

After Margaret died he married fast,
a pretty woman from the town —
for the children's sake.

Bliss at first and games of love.
He woke each morning lost
in the midnight of her hair.

One night he said "Quiet, sweetness,
you'll wake the children."
Her eyes clouded over.

Next morning, eyes still cloudy,
she told him to "do something"
about the kids.

The love games stopped until he took
the children, Hansel and Gretel,
into the forest and returned without them.

When she asked if this dress made her ass look fat,
he answered wrong and hardly ever again
woke lost in the midnight of her hair.

The children are OK, thanks. Gretel works
at Taco Bell, and Hansel works in retail sales —
in another part of the forest.

Bitter Vetch

She shattered me with her smile, almost distracting my attention from her **36 across**.

I stammered something stupid like, "Hello, **18 down**, is this your first time here?"

"No," she said, "I come here sometimes with my **56 down**, usually after a game."

"Can I get you something to drink, an **8 across** or a cold beer?"
"No thanks, I'll hold off for awhile until my **56 down** gets here."
I nodded, understanding, ate some peanuts and finished my **17 down**.

Soon, a ripple of sound from the folks by the door as a gigantic man entered. It was George **13 across**, halfback for the **42 down**.

He worked the crowd a little then ploughed over to the gal with the shattering smile.

"Hi doll," he said. "Let's blow this place and go to dinner. I'm hungry."

"Sure," she said — looking at me. "This joint **29 across** and is starting to bore the **7 down** out of me."

They exited gracefully through the crowd.

I ordered another **17 down**, congratulating myself that I hadn't pressed the gal with the shattering smile — and the gorgeous **36 across**.

Born Again Tap Dancer

Ever notice that in some former life
most folks were kings
or queens or tribal chieftains
or grand poobahs?

Not me.

More than likely I was
a mosquito up in Alaska. Or maybe
a giant clam, snug at the bottom
of a topaz bay, south of Bora Bora.

I passed some mystical exam, and
after death, was promoted to a human.
Now, here I am, like a Brownie
who "flew up" to become a Girl Scout.

On most counts this is better than
being a mosquito or a giant clam.
The diet is more varied and there's
greater access to classical music.

If I pass my next mid-terms I'll learn
to tap dance. I can't do that now,
and I couldn't as a mosquito or
as a giant clam, either

Early Haircut

Acres of white tile. Six barbers standing by huge chairs smiling.
Dad nods to one who begins to smile less
as he installs a child's seat.

I'm lifted. Then a band of crepe paper is put around my neck
and a large striped sheet covers all but my head.

Dad tells the barber what to do and pats me on the shoulder.
Then he settles into a chair and lights a cigar.

Millions of mirrors and millions of barbers.
Millions of dads and millions of me.
We're in a green glass box stretching forever
getting smaller and smaller.

The millions of barbers move together, so do the million me's.
"Don't squirm young man." His fingers touch my shoulder
without real menace — I guess because dad is there — watching.

I'm combed and clippered and scissored and combed again.
And sprayed and brushed. And then —
a mirror is held before my face.

I don't know what to say. Dad says it for me.
"He looks like a movie star." Then we go for ice cream.

Barber shops have changed a lot.
And so have I.
Yet, when barbers ask me, "How would you like it?"
I answer, "Make me look like a movie star."

Failing English

"The high school called.
You've got to meet with his counselor.
He's failing English."

I waited in the office. The counselor was busy.

A bearded man greeted a young lady sorting mail.
"Wow, Claire — great shoes! Where'dja get 'em at?"
"These? I got em at the 'Foot Locker' last week."

After he left I asked her, "Who was that?"
"Who was what?"
"The man who asked you where you got your shoes at."

Two black caterpillars hugged at the bridge of her nose
then she smiled and shrugged.
"Oh yeah, where I got em at. Not to worry,"
she said conspiratorially,
"he's a History teacher."

Father Knew Napoleon

On a small French farm, close to Maginot Line, is an
ordinary man with ordinary wife and kids.
Yet, neighbors swear they see an aura 'round him
sometimes. They nod wise heads and watch this man
descended from the man whose father knew Napoleon.

He has rejected public office many times. He won't let
others stand him drinks. This private, lofty stance keeps
honor burnished. It is a family trait of the man
whose father knew Napoleon.

How well did father know Napoleon?
Did they share a cognac?
Was he on the emperor's staff?

How could he walk in dignity if neighbors knew the truth?
He sighs and thinks a thousandth time,
"Ah, how I wish he knew Napoleon under other circumstances."

The truth is this — Father saw the emperor
with a small entourage. They paused there, by the stone wall.
Napoleon swung out of the saddle and urinated on the wall. He
adjusted his breeches, turned and smiled at father. "Good day,"
he said with a strange accent. He mounted again and the small
band rode off to that tree line where the road curves to the west.

Father had put his cap back on
and, wrapped in an envelope of glory, sat on a log
to savor the memory.
Soon after that — his son became the man
whose father knew Napoleon.

I Want to Be a Pirate

I loathe algebra and Trig-i-nom-etry
I want to be a pirate and sail on the deep blue sea.
Yes a PIRATE, a PIRATE
that's what I want to be.

Pirates needn't brush their teeth or eat their broccoli
they pig out on ice cream and chicken fricassee
they sleep in late and never bathe.
They live like a VIP.

A PIRATE, a PIRATE, that's what I want to be.

I'll have a wooden leg and a steel hook for a hand
and roll in wealth in best of health in a hearty pirate band.
I'll wear velvet pants and a shirt with frills
with pockets for gold and my seasick pills.

A PIRATE, a PIRATE, that's what I want to be.

You can be a banker or practice philanthropy,
but I want to be a pirate, that's what I want to be.
I'll wear an earring in my ear and drink the best Chablis
as a hairy, scary PIRATE out on the deep blue sea.

A PIRATE, a PIRATE, that's what I want to be.

It Ain't Gonna Happen in Memphis

He told me that he loved me
and other sugar lies.
He held me close and whispered
and blinked his bedroom eyes.

"Let's slip away to Memphis,
a weekend would be fine.
You'll open up your heart to me
and I will open mine."

I smiled and pushed his hands away
and said, "No sir, not me.
It ain't gonna happen in Memphis,
in Memphis, Tennessee.

"You might tempt me with Shanghai.
Or Rome or gay Pareee,
but it ain't gonna happen in Memphis,
in Memphis, Tennessee."

He sighed and said we'd party some
and drink expensive wine
'cause way down south in Memphis
things are oh so fine.

Then I replied, "Listen Clyde.
It ain't gonna happen in Memphis,
leastwise not to me,
drinking muscatel in some cheap motel
in Memphis, in Memphis, Tennessee.

"You don't stand a chance
of getting in my pants
in Memphis, in Memphis, Tennessee."

Leaving Home

In the evening, when it was cool, God walked in the garden.
He saw their footprints, saw they had been rolling in the grass.
Saw the skins and stems of the fruit, smelled the sex.

They were hiding in the bushes, happy.
They had never known unhappiness.
"God is out there, probably making up new rules," he said.
She smiled and whispered, "Quiet, he'll hear you."
God called, "Come out, I know you're in there. Come out and listen to me."
They walked from the bushes and stood under the stars, in front of God.

"I've raised you and tried to teach you to be responsible adults,
I've given you a good home life, I've given you the whole world.
In the beginning you were good children.
But lately, you've been disobedient and rebellious."
They frowned and hung their heads.

"I understand all that – you're growing up.
But now, it's no more 'Mister Nice Guy.'
Now it's time for you to be on your own.
On Monday I want you out of here.
Get a job, get a life, find your own place to live.
I'll visit sometimes, to see that you're all right."

They nodded sadly. He hugged them both.
There were tears.
On Monday they were gone.

Little Bit of Ernie

Ernie was sort of funny in the head.
He told the little kids there was no Santa Claus and later
the facts of life — both barrels.
The kids wouldn't talk to their folks for weeks.

Ernie looked angelic. He stole from his mom,
from school lockers. Drugstores.
At twelve he smoked a pack a day
and drank vodka — neat.

Ernie put dirty pictures into library books,
and felt up girls at high school dances.
He was mean but never violent
and was never caught.

Then I heard he'd beaten up
his girlfriend, Joanne — broke her arm,
split her lip and blackened both her eyes.

"What the hell, Ernie, why?" I asked him.
He shook his head and pursed his lips.
"She lost the cigarette lighter I gave her,
the special cigarette lighter."

I remembered that lighter —
covered in tanned leather.
How he smiled all attentive, kind and loving
each time she lit a cigarette.

Unaware he'd been circumcised at eighteen or
the leather covered lighter she'd lost was
a little bit of Ernie.

Lost and Found

Something's lost at our house and mama's worried.
No smiles or cooking smells — and all us kids scurrying
looking in drawers and under cushions for the lost
lottery ticket, cornerstone of mama's financial plan.

She's lit candles on Saint Anthony's shelf.
"Find it Antonio. We need it."
Anthony seems sad in the candlelight, holding baby Jesus.
"Pay attention kids, He's trying to tell you where it is."
Nodding, stomachs knotted, we keep looking —
in books, under the tea tray, in with the dish towels.

Then comes real pressure — Mama takes baby Jesus
from Anthony and hides him in her underwear drawer!
There'll be cold food tonight.
Don't even think about dessert. No TV. No radio.
Do your homework and keep looking for the lottery ticket.

We've looked most places twice or more.
Then, Michael whoops from the hall,
"Found it – inside the umbrella!"
Mama smiles, slaps her head – "I put it there
to keep it safe – then forgot."
She smiles, "Thank you dear Antonio."

Crossing herself, she blows out candles
and returns baby Jesus to Anthony's arms.
Soon — the sounds of pots and pans, and TV;
and Dolores, on the telephone again.

Saint Anthony, on the shelf
holding baby Jesus,
still looks sad.
He knows the ticket's
not a winner.

Misfortune Cookies

I have never opened a Misfortune Cookie.
Yet, in a rational world
misfortune cookies must exist.

Silver linings
must have clouds.
Every Yang must a Yin.

Tonight my fortune read
*You will be offered a high executive position
with an attractive salary.*

Somebody's cookie must have
condemned him to work in a sweatshop
for less than minimum wage.

If your cookie says
*You will always get what you want
through your charm and personality.*

Somewhere a cookie tells a poor chump,
*Lacking charm and personality,
you will never get what you want.*

Moses was a Dog Person

Moses was a dog person.
I suspect Mrs. Moses was not.
At any rate, his dog followed Moses and the Chosen People
out of Egypt two steps ahead of the Pharaoh's soldiers.

Moses had a succession of dogs. All of them were poodles.
Not French Poodles of course (France hadn't been invented yet)
but poodles all the way back to Noah.
He called each of his poodles "Henri" (or Henry, if you prefer).

Moses was rarely seen without his dog.
Wandering forty years in the desert before finding the Promised
Land was mostly because Henri just had to sniff every rock,
every bush, every aloe plant. If Moses had a leash
the whole thing would have been much faster.

When Moses climbed Sinai to receive the ten commandments,
Henri was at his side (sometimes even dashing ahead). It is a little
known fact that the Lord also gave some commandments to Henri.

Only four, because it is hard for some dogs to remember more
than that. The four dog commandments are: Heel, Sit, Fetch
and Roll Over.

Dogs who obey these commandments will go to heaven.
Dogs in heaven? You bet — what sort of a place
would heaven be without dogs?

(Joel thanked his friend/poet John Pray for the idea)

Now What?

He was always "out of focus," she thought.
Soon after they were married he threw himself into chess,
with abandon.

When that white heat cooled it was martial arts
with judo clothes and a sword.

He explored the fringes of yoga
with its graceful asanas, mudras and mantras.
Somehow he was sure that he could levitate
if only he could meditate — properly.

Then, oil painting — portable easel, floppy hat,
rustle of expensive brushes, haunting smell of terps.

Next — the Rosacrucians, A.M.O.R.C.
Followed by writing and publishing
his own poetry.

So now, when she caught sight of the bright green
shamrock tattooed two inches below his ancient belly button,
she couldn't help but ask herself,
"Now what?"

Reclining Woman

Transfixed, I studied the photograph of a reclining woman,
her back to the camera, jaw-droppingly beautiful,
naked as a peeled apple.

Now, the purported origin of the Trojan War
seemed plausible. Men would slaughter
to capture and possess her.

The photograph explored her body as a basilica, caressing
her shoulders, arpeggioing down the white keys of her spine,
celebrating her buttocks. She was evidence God must love us.

Turning to leave the gallery I saw a tall woman regarding me.
I'm sure she thought, "Eat your heart out, you old goat."
Not a bull's-eye, but not much off target.

Things of Value

She held the fabric, felt its smoke-like lack of weight
and asked her chamberlain, "Is this a thing of value?"

Such questions seemed more frequent now.

"Majesty, the value of a thing depends on many factors.
In our land we have cotton, linen and wool for
clothing, tents, and sacks and sails;
but nothing such as this rare fabric brought
from the east by traders. This fabric seems to have
no real substance. I don't know what its use may be.
Its value seems to be in its rarity."

"So the value of a thing lies in its rarity?"

He smiled, "Yes, majesty. Usually rarity,
sometimes also the wisdom a thing conveys,
its usefulness, and sometimes surely the pleasure it brings."

"It pleases me — its color and its lightness.
I value it and will find some use for it."

Piece by piece, aided by the chamberlain
and her trusted servants, she collected things of value.
Rare objects, things that pleased her. A delicate cup,
a favorite chair, a toy from childhood, a statue of her cat,
carvings, gem stones. She had strands of the
valued silk fabric woven into her hair.

All her valued things were placed in her tomb.
The trusted servants are there too.
All except her valued chamberlain who had
the good sense to be up river on a matter of state
before the queen chose which valued things
would accompany her into eternity.

Spotless

Spotless. That's how I was,
or felt I was. Spotless.

When I was five my tiny misdeeds
didn't leave a stain.

As a young godlet I played
with my spotless godlet friends.

Life was milk and cookies,
warm smiles, sweetness.

Sin arrived at seven
when I learned that
Adam and Eve's misbehavior had
bubbled up through the myriad "begats"
to engulf me and
my immaculate playmates.

We were all polluted in the stink
and stain of original sin.

I haven't felt spotless
since then. And
I miss feeling spotless.

Love Poems

> First light in the East
> Rooster, having done his job
> Turns to thoughts of love.
>
> Haiku, Joel Fallon

Although Joel and Carolyn knew each other's families and had school friends in common, they never met while in school. Then, one Christmas in 1950, they both went caroling with a group of friends, but they only had eyes for each other. I asked Carolyn if it was love at first sight. She smiled and said, "It was more like lust at first sight." He asked her to marry him two days later.

Her mother was not amused. She didn't want her bridge club to know that her twenty-and-a-half-year-old daughter wanted to marry a nineteen-year-old soldier, and a private at that. She insisted that they wait until Joel turned a respectable twenty years of age. They did wait, but just barely, the wedding taking place mere days after his June 16, 1951, birthday.

The result was a marriage that lasted for sixty-five years.

Their ardor never waned.

Did You?

Did you hear far-off thunder in the night
and then the whisper of the rain?

Did you come to me silently in early morning darkness
and lie beside me?

Did you push aside the sheet
and caress away the years?

Did you press your lips to my shoulder
and give me your breasts?

If not you,
who the hell was that?

Clean Sheets, Dirty Woman

The garden was hot and green that afternoon.
I read and dozed, wishing she were with me
instead of in the hot green garden.
After an eternity or two the screen door clapped.
Then her light step on the porch and the sound of
her shears, touching the wall, hung
in her apron pocket.

Steps again, then silence.
I turned to see her smile-lit face,
smudged and glistening moistly.
Our eyes touched and she stepped from the pool
her garden clothes had made around her.

She smelled of tomatoes — do you know that smell?
And rosemary and mint and other dark
musky sweet stuff, deep in the matrix of the earth,
down where the seeds and roots are found.

We touched and smiled and laughed
and, as the hot green afternoon
ripened into evening, we were one,
a number
of times.

He Caught a Glimpse of Her

He caught a glimpse of her
in lingerie at Montgomery Ward.
She smiled.
Caught by lust or love, he
averted his eyes and went upstairs to
Sporting Goods.
Later, from his Studebaker,
he saw her again.

That summer they danced.
Lust or love compressed their
views of the world.
It got steamy in her Packard
Clipper.

That fall they married.
She became a splendid cook.
He built a Heathkit radio that
served them well for years.

Kids and schools, and bridge,
and more complex projects,
built with parts from Radio Shack.

Some things
never end.

Remember Bougainvillea

I remember summer
in the garden,
late afternoon, after swimming.
Warm adobe walls and
we are alone in the bougainvillea arbor.

Thorns on brown limbs
in green shadow.
Scarlet blooms
in your hands
and dark thorns on your pale
adobe breasts.

You frown when a thorn
draws dark blood.
I kiss the taste of blood
and kiss your sharp dark thorns.

I remember you in summer.
I remember bougainvillea.

Running in the Louvre

Imagine running in the Louvre
some rainy afternoon —
racing down the echoing halls,
past Pietas, Rembrandts and Bruegels.

Pound up the marble stairs to see
enamels, bronze and cloisonné,
the Mona Lisa's haunting face,
the Victory of Samothrace.

Run past jewels and precious stones,
gallop past Egyptian bones —
a treasure house of graceful things
left to us by ancient kings.

An afternoon of running in the Louvre
leaves grace and beauty just a senseless blur.
A lifetime of loving you is just like that —
like running in the Louvre.

Swiss Army Knife

Slippery as a trout, slender,
smelling like
piña colada,
she smiles
and steps from the shower.

Later, wrapped in terry cloth,
sitting on a deck chair
in the eucalyptus shadow,
she gazes at me with
burnt umber eyes.

She smiles, "What would you do
if I asked you to cut off your arm?"
I leave her
to find my
Swiss army knife.

Love Power

Love makes me want:
to have my teeth fixed,
lose twenty pounds,
rent a motel room,
buy a violin and learn to play it,
take tango lessons.

And if she loves me I'll:
make every day a Sunday for her,
hold her hand,
clean up my damn vocabulary,
try to be a better person,
buy new underwear.

Love in the Kitchen

She is nimble in the kitchen
preparing early dinner.
Sugar, half teaspoon in the wooden bowl,
to diffuse the clove of garlic rubbed in circles
in the bowl.

Her apron says "KISS THE COOK."
I long to do so.
The salad comes together
magically.

Apron and light dress do not conceal the
fluid movement nor mask the beauty of her form.
We sip a glass of plonk.

She prepares tomato sauce with speed and grace.
Bringing water to a boil, she adds oil and a pinch of salt
then the pasta.

There is a sheen on her forehead.
She smiles and removes the garlic bread
from the oven.

I am undone and love her.
I've acquired an appetite and can't bear
to sit here much longer without
eating her spaghetti
straps.

Zinfandel Smile

Birds don't take voice lessons.
I think she didn't either.
Yet, she sang so freely and with such joy
the birds were shamed.

Falling in love,
I watched her sing —
with half closed, smoky eyes,
brown throat, smiling now.
Now
not smiling.

Dark hair in her eyes
dark lashes
long.
Head thrown back,
parted lips.

If she smiles her zinfandel smile at me
I will mow her lawn,
muck out her stables and
dig her well
forever.

Key Lime Pie

I met a gal, oh me, oh my,
she was prim and sorta shy.

I kissed her an' ***I like to die,***
she tasted just like key lime pie!

Key lime pie, Key lime pie
I sing yer praises to the sky.

I've had apple, cherry, la-la Berry
Mince or punkin' pie and I don't give a dang
about lemon meringue
I want key lime pie.

I said – You be my gal, I'll be yer guy
if you let me taste your key lime pie.
Then sure enough she let me try
a little bit of key lime pie.

We don't want apple, cherry, la-la Berry
mince or punkin' pie and we don't give a dang
about lemon meringue
we want key lime pie.

Now we'll be together until we die,
living on love and key lime pie.

I Remember You

I remember you and
how at night
your eyes caught stars, and
how you whispered
words of the songs
from across the lake.

I remember you and
how your hands
moved in my hands and
the paper lanterns
dappled shadows of leaves
on your arms.

I remember you and
freckles on your cheeks and
how your eyes searched mine,
memorizing me
and how you smiled sadly
when the dance was done.

Perhaps Then

When all the bowls have cracked
and silver has been polished to a memory,
and light has traveled
twice to earth from far Antares,

when fearful weapons' half-lives
have expired
and tanks and guns in rusty mounds
lie useless,

when body's every molecule
has been sloughed off like
snake skin
leaving only fingerprints unchanged,

perhaps then,
unlikely as it seems,
I may start
to love you less.

Pillow Talk

Quarter to four, in bed the old couple
hold hands and talk quietly
about last night's dinner, about who
will help their daughter
execute their will,

How to improve the wooden stairs to the basement
(paint versus linoleum),
how to move the stone fountain they bought
at a garage sale back to their house.
He says he'll borrow a neighbor's truck,

She thinks it'll fit in their hatchback.
He says, let's go back to sleep, okay?
Silence for a few moments,
then she says, "I'm going to buy sesame seeds."
He breaks into laughter.

Love Letter

Dark attic. Forgotten trunk, a letter,
dated late 1800's, found in a book,
to "My Rose" his love, from TH, my grandfather,
before they married.

Bold words in a strong hand recalling
past meetings, sketching plans for the future.
And soft, caressing words a lover whispers
into his lover's ear.

Then, lightning bolts, stark intimate, bedroom
words impossible to think my grandma knew.
Yet, there they were, written to her,
saved in the attic.

She remembered birthdays, and baked lazy daisy cakes.
She bought me coloring books, and she saved this letter.
I put it back. Perhaps I'll read it again after I get used
to knowing we're both grown up.

Apple Wind

Apple wind at evening,
soft, from the west,
threading through the valley.

Before light fades,
trout
rise to small insects.

Prayers said and water drunk,
the children are tucked in.
Then,

man and woman on the porch
are lightly wrapped in Beethoven
and soft apple wind.

Drive Safely

Alone in the car between home and work
he says her name twice and smiles.
Somewhere she is thinking "drive safely love."

Perhaps if drivers knew that someone
loved them, really loved them,
they'd all drive safely.

On Poetry

As you have seen by now, Joel was not a poet in the "classical" sense. His form was his own eclectic mix of breath lines, internal and (sometimes) end rhymes, and prose poems — all delivered with the precision of a skilled orator.

His poem "The Golden Owl," page 117, expresses that style best.

A Poet Passes
remembering Robert Shelby

The poet put a shine on things
and tidied up the way we see them.

He polished old truths until
we reflected on them.

The poet had at least a hundred ways
to make us change our mind,

to laugh out loud and yes,
to break our hearts.

Poem on a Napkin

Poem on a napkin
Last Supper on an egg shell
Toothpick Eiffel Tower

Under a short leg
Steadying the table
My latest chapbook

Ideas are real.
Things
Are not.

New Poem

My new poem waits like a bride
and I hurry home to
my beloved.

I touch her lean flanks
with my hot
hands

and kiss the secret places between
her smooth
stanzas.

Belly to belly we discover
new pleasures again,
and again.

Reconstruction

I built a poem last night,
then slept on it.

This morning, early —
I nudged and worried
the defenseless thing.

Then, I disassembled it
and sat with pieces
scattered out before me.

I buffed and burnished parts
and slowly, Lego-like,
put it back together.

There are some parts
left over.

Sometimes a Poem

Sometimes a poem will grab you
by the arm and tug you into a dingy doorway,
or whisper in your ear about the strangest things
or, smiling, sink gleaming fangs into your throat.

And while you're walking in a barren landscape,
sometimes a poem will sidle up next to you,
match your step and begin
talking softly or humming.

Sometimes a poem lies
incomplete and unfulfilled
in poetic purgatory,
waiting for the coup de grâce.

Sometimes a poem cannot be satisfied
until she sucks the marrow from your bones,
and leaves you gasping with
your thesaurus unzipped.

Poetry Zoo

On such a lovely day you should
take the children to the zoo —
the poetry zoo

to watch the stately odes wading in the water
with grey clouds scudding over,
to hear their plaintive cry,
they're almost extinct.

Kids love the brilliant feathers and chattering
of the Taiwanese sestinas. At first they were homesick
but the keepers started speaking Mandarin to them
and everything straightened out.

Don't miss the Italian sonnets striding behind bars
in their cage, whispering to themselves —
long claws clicking on the concrete.

Avoid the nasty limericks.
They shout filth and throw feces
from their cages.
Disgusting.

A baby pantoum was born here last year.
He's almost fully grown now.
Children enjoy his awkward oinks.

With the shape the world is in poems may soon be gone.
Take youngsters to the poetry zoo now, before it's too late.
Let them see and hear an important part of their heritage.

Castaway Companion

Who would I choose to sit with me
beneath the lofty banyan,
to share a desert island
as a castaway companion?

Someone who learned survival skills
from Arapahos or Pawnees
or who had memorized
all of Aristophanes.

I've rejected Madame Bovary,
Columbus, Galileo.
Passed over Bellefonte
with incessant cries of, "Day Oh."

I think I'm done with dancing girls
who shake their lusty tushes,
although it might be fun
to drag one to the bushes.

Now, after all
is said and done
I think I choose for all 'round fun
the lovely Emily Dickenson.

Around the fire she'd weave such poems
the crabs and fish would leave their homes.
With shells and scales glistening
they'd sit around us listening.

We'd find flat stones for skipping,
indulge in skinny dipping.
Emily, Oh Emily we'd get along so well.
If you would be my heaven, I'd try not to be your hell.

The Golden Owl

"Make a poem like this," he said,
then showed me how to fit it together
like a golden owl,
vowels round and plump,
every feather sculpted,
and, in each amber eye, forever.

Intricate and precious too,
but the words were jiggered 'round
to fit some ancient pattern and
ideas got fuzzed and fizzled out.

"That owl won't fly." I told him.
He smiled and said, "I know.

"If you take a baby's foot
natural and functional,
then break it, fold its toes under.
Mutilate it in the name of beauty.
You know damn well
such feet can't walk.
And this golden owl can't fly
because it is caged in a cruel format
in the name of beauty.

"Be god to your poem.
Focus on ideas instead of format.
Beauty happens when
feet walk and golden owls fly
free."

Leave Some Silence

Leave some silence,
some emptiness in your life,
your conversation, your poems.

Sounds are not continuous.
In conversation there must be pauses.
There must be room for thoughts to form.

In an empty apartment,
let others choose some furniture
and figure where to place it.

Make your life,
your conversation, your poems
cooperative efforts.

Let others paddle
for a while. You'll be pleased,
so will they.

The Taste of Poetry

I savor Sandburg's stuff —
honest meat and potatoes, lots of rich gravy
and apple pie with coffee.

Breakfast with Bukowski is pizza,
cold the morning after,
with a bottle of beer, deciding not
to shave, and smoking a Camel
in the kitchen.

Billy Collins satisfies like corned beef
with hot mustard and soda bread —
and a decent pudding with Irish coffee
while a tenor sings ***The Bard of Armagh***
so sweet 'twould bring tears to a stone.

Yes, give me a poet whose work is tasty
and sticks to my ribs.
And you can keep your haiku
for appetizers.

Poets' Show and Tell

Every then and now
souls gather for show and tell.
Conspiracies of poets' souls
drag bodies to cafés and
coffee shops to breathe together
the air of poetry.

We show and tell truths
found while to'ing, fro'ing
or merely sitting silently.
New shiny truths just found, and
old truths rediscovered.

Hold up a truth for all to see
how light makes it sparkle when
you turn it, hear it, touch it, rub it.

Other truths too terrible to gaze on.
Black holes engulf all matter, light and sanity.
Avert your eyes — or turn to salt.
Listen only — cautiously.

Cafés and coffee houses
then and now — are universities
where souls
learn truth at show and tell.

No One Here

I sat in here the other night
drinking tea and
leafing through
a book of poems.

A woman entered,
looked around, then
called back through
the open door, "There's no one here."

No one here?
Odds are I danced
with her mother
when we were both fifteen.

And later surfed the white hot lava of her love
then, maybe barefoot, stood
out in the snow
of her distain.

Perhaps her dad and I
shared a canteen and
laughed at Maggie's drawers
out on the rifle range.

I'm no geranium sitting here
under the neon's hum.
I still can surf love's glowing lava
and yet may squeeze a poem or two
from this old withered brain.

Joel at his last Bencicia Poet's Picnic
August, 2016

Endings

All poets, from time to time, write about the ending of things — love affairs, marriages, friendships, death. In the last years of his life Joel suffered the effects of liver cancer. Carolyn said it was ironic that he contracted sclerosis of the liver, because at age fifty he had sworn off alcohol. I asked him once why he didn't drink when we went out. He replied that, "A drink became a bottle and a bottle became a case" and he didn't want to go there again.

One of his last e-mails to his poet friends reflects his particular mix of humor and common sense. "Well," he said "it doesn't look like I'm going to get out of this alive after all." True to form, his last outing with other poets was to a reading in Alameda where he, again, held court.

Japanese Death Poems

(by Zen Monks and Haiku Poets on the verge of death)

1.
Today is the day
for one last view of
Mount Fuji.

KIMPO
3 September 1894

2.
I cast the brush aside —
From here on I'll speak to the
Moon face to face.

KOHA
14 August, 1897

Tuman (The Mist)*

The wind was soft.
It barely stirred the mist
gathered under the shoulder
of the Presidio.

My father and I
watched from the garrison
as your ship made
silent progress westward
past the Island of Pelicans;

watched until it disappeared
into the mist at the mouth
of our lovely bay.

Who will walk with me now
under the pines?

Who will teach me French
and dance with me?

Who will whisper
"Krasivaya Moya" to me
now that you have disappeared
into the mist?

---

*This poem commemorates ill-fated love between Concepción Argüello, daughter of the commandant of the Presidio, and Nikolai Rezanov, a Russian nobleman. He perished on a trip back to Russia to gain permission from his church to marry. Concepción then chose to become the first native-born nun in California and taught school at St Catherine's in Benicia. She died in 1857 and is buried in St. Dominic's cemetery in Benicia.

On Grandma's Chair

The chair, of course,
was Grandma Kate's.
The basin? I don't know.

The flowers,
drenched in golden sun,
are presents for our river town.

Mid-summer children
out of school,
have no time for flowers.

But old folks smile to see them
blazing in the basin, there,
on grandma's chair.

*(An Ekphrastic poem based upon the painting
"Rich's Chair" by Pat Ryll)*

Toy Top

The toy top had a red wood handle
on a twisted metal ribbon that you
worked up and down and up and down
to set it spinning and singing.

When you stopped pumping, the brilliant colors
blurred and blended – shimmering as the top spun
and sang a top song –
whirling on the hardwood floor.

When the toy top slowed
the singing became faint.
When the singing stopped the top
teetered and fell over.

I've spun for a while
now my singing's getting faint.
Sometimes I teeter;
falling over must be coming next.

Property Disposal

The funeral is arranged,
no ritual expected.
Most of our goods are spoken for.

We're comfortable with that.
 Books, pictures, furniture all have
destinations.

The silver?
Perhaps they'll draw straws.
We hate to break up the set.

A child asks, "Grandpa, when will I get your sword?"
I tell him, "Pretty soon now,
pretty soon."

Old Clocks

When it's quiet,
I close my eyes and
remember the sound of a
clock in my childhood.
Enamel face with downcast eyes,
brass pendulum and weights
of dull brass too.
Grandmother Roe saw to winding the clock.
When she died, the clock disappeared under the waves
in a flood wash of relatives.
Then, I hear the ticking of another clock, the beautiful clock
we rescued from a sad pile of clock corpses
in the attic of a German antique dealer.
We took it home and brought it back to life.
It ticked for decades until,
as an old man, I gave it to my son lest it also
disappear under some waves in a flood wash of relatives.

I Buy Rare Cars

That is to say, when I buy a new car it is rare.
More precisely, I rarely buy a new car.
Every car I've ever owned looked "paid for,"
even the two or three new ones.

Last week ended my fifteen-year relationship
with a car I bought new. After two hundred
thousand miles, her wrinkles couldn't be
hidden any more.

Her heart was still sturdy but her upholstery was shot.
She needed a paint job, new exhaust system,
a rebuilt air conditioner, new lights, and new tires —
the whole enchilada.

Even after expensive reconstruction she'd
stand out like a tart at noon and seem suspiciously
ancient by candlelight. Odometers can be
turned back; clocks cannot.

Together we knocked about Germany, Italy and France
and crossed the States a few times. We savored miles
and kilometers with equal gusto. Autobahns,
Autostrada, Turnpikes, toll roads — we knew them all.

And, we took care of each other.
She carried me to the hospital for blood tests
and diabetes problems. I brought her in for brakes, a new
clutch, alternator and many sets of high speed Michelins.

Shabby, disheveled, I couldn't bear to put her down —
to pull her feeding tube. I donated her to charity hoping
she'd be reborn, refurbished to become a sturdy
taxi in Nigeria, where folks can't afford rare cars either.

Karma Work

Look back at yesterdays
piled on yesterdays.
Strip away the layers.

Recall rules broken, charities withheld,
kind words unsaid.
What do they weigh?

A card touched is a card played.
The detonator activates the main charge.
Megatons of karma explode.

Undo cruelty. Overcome neglect.
Say, "I love you" often – and mean it.
Recycle and stop pissing in the pool.

Family Resemblance

Diabetes, and his noncompliant nature,
toyed awhile with my kid brother,
took his leg, then killed him.
A bad death it was.

Diabetes asks me to play.
My answer, "No thanks, not today."
I mind my manners, take my meds.
My brother watches.

Diabetes doesn't go away.
It tests, and probes and changes me.
My doctor and I speak Chinese.
Perhaps, together, we can fool it.

Diabetes puzzles at first
over my new meds. Then smiles
in recognition.
My soul asks my body, "Is that you?"

Diabetes watches,
behind every mirror,
searching for
a family resemblance.

Drying Dishes

Perhaps "drying" is the wrong word.
She stands beside the dishwasher
removing clean plates and glasses and cups and
spoons, and puts them on the counter. Drying
only when she must.

"This handsome plate from Soufflenheim," she smiles,
"and this graceful piece of silver,
Repousse."
It had survived the San Francisco 'quake and fire.

"Which of these plates and cups and spoons
will be on my table when I die?"
She touches old favorites, speaking softly to herself.

"I hope this cup — and this plate too instead of ..."

Her lips don't say the words. Squeezing eyes
to shut from sight an older self.

Unvisited.

Tied by a dirty apron into a wheelchair,
fed with plastic spoon from a soulless
plastic plate
by a gruff obese Serbo-Croatian woman
with wild hair.

I Am Still

I am still
the child in the pool –
slim and quick and tan, squinting at the sun.

I am still
an ordinary seaman in the bosun's chair
with bucket and brush, depending on a pineapple hitch.

I am still
the recruit, dressed right and covered down,
with dog tags, assembling a rifle
under a poncho.

I am still
learning the kirillitsa, ingesting chunks of vocabulary,
unscrambling the instrumental case.

I am still
loudly singing songs remembered
from grammar school.

I am still
all of those, yet – often now,
as light fades,
I sit alone and
I am still.

Ready or Not

Ready or not,
I shall be caught
some day.

Perhaps today
will be the day
that I die.

Already there's more rind than melon
and I can see the bottom
of the glass.

I'll avoid loud sounds of sucking
through a soda straw. Sweetness dies,
and then it's gone.

Surrounded by family
or kicked to death in an alley
by someone's grandson.

Ready or not,
I shall be caught,
some day.

The Lifting Team

Recently in the hospital,
and in great pain
from broken bones
after an accident,
I had to be lifted:
bed to gurney, gurney to
x-ray table (brutally hard), table to chair.

Each time they sent for the Lifting Team:
Solomon, built like a football player with
a wide smile, and Merwin, smaller, agile,
a savvy bird. Each time Solomon would say
(seeing the tenseness of fear on my face),
"Don't worry, you'll be alright."
Indeed, their arms held me in a firm cocoon,
I never felt the slightest pain.

When in death's last delirium,
I shall call on the Lifting Team,
they will arrive as angels at my bedside;
and Solomon will say, "Don't worry, you'll be alright."
And they will halt my ghastly nose-dive into hell,
and lift me up, up, high up
into the fields of stars.

A Ghost Story

Life will end, that is clear.
What happens then is not clear.

If there are options, I'd like to be a ghost.
Maybe I could talk to other ghosts.

To thank my father's ghost,
for his loving kindness.

To tell my sister's ghost how I really tried
to see her before she died, but failed.

To shake the ghostly hands of soldiers
who died much too early.

To apologize to legions of other ghosts
for having withheld my love.

Where the Snowmen Go

When it is over,
please no splash or show,
just say I went away
to where the snowmen go.

Photo by Peter Bray

Goodbye, Joel. I hope you found all your ghosts and told them what you needed to say. It's only a matter of time until I join you some heavenly Tuesday, to read together again...

Afterword

I hope that you enjoyed reading this book of Joel's poems as much as I did compiling it. It was a challenge. Joel was not a "conventional" or "traditional" poet. Eclectic might be a good description. He tended to sprinkle his poems with long lines, almost prose, and let the word processing program chop them up based on its own rules. He also treated his poems as works in progress, so there were multiple versions of each to review and ponder.

He was considerate though, leaving enough punctuation, misspellings, and other composition questions to reward my review and editing, and to make me feel I contributed something to his works.

In preparing this book, talking with his wife Carolyn and reviewing all of his writings I could get my hands on, I gained a greater regard for Joel and a deeper feeling for the friendship he always displayed. One that I share with all of those other friends he made and cultivated along the way.

In this book, Joel came alive for me once more. In reading it, I hope you had that experience too.

Sincerely,
Don Peery

Alphabetic Index of Poems

	(page)
21 Hayes to Shangri-La	72
Another Part of the Forest	75
Anti-Tank Team	26
Apple Wind	108
Apples and Worms	44
Artillery Training, a Day Well spent	25
Banned in Benicia	74
Best Day, Worst Day	7
Bitter Vetch	76
Bonus	12
Born Again Tap Dancer	77
Care and Cleaning	23
Castaway Companion	116
Clean Sheets, Dirty Woman	95
Cloud Children	56
Coach and Pupil	24
Coming Home	28
Conversion	57
Cut Away Man, The	43
Day He Died, The	65
Detective Story	47
Did You?	94
Digging to China	2
Dirty Diaper Lie	4
Do Pigs Win?	58
Drive Safely	109
Drying Dishes	133

Early Haircut	78
Eucalyptus, The	41
Explosive Ordnance	30
Failing English	79
Family Resemblance	132
Father Knew Napoleon	80
Flying Fish	14
Ghost Story, A	137
Golden Owl, The	117
Green Street Marching Band, The	40
He Caught a Glimpse of Her	96
High Crime or Misdemeanor	70
I Am Still	134
I Buy Rare Cars	130
I Forget the Name of the Girl	71
I Remember You	104
I Walked Again on the Beach Today	37
I Want to Be a Pirate	81
In Korea	31
Infinite Shades of Blue	15
It Ain't Gonna Happen in Memphis	82
Japanese Death Poems	124
Jumping Ship	19
Karma Work	131
Key Lime Pie	103
Laundromat	39
Leave Some Silence	118
Leaving Home	83
Lifeboat	13
Lifting Team, The	136
Lilac Vegetal	9
Little Bit of Ernie	84
Lost and Found	85

Love in the Kitchen	101
Love Letter	107
Love Power	100
Man is There, A	55
Man of Consequence, A	73
Manila Bay	17
Marginalia	50
Mean Man, The	4
Mercy of October	45
Mid-East Questions	59
Misfortune Cookies	86
Mister Baraban Forgives God	44
Moses was a Dog Person	87
Mountain Woman	45
My Town	36
Naked Ladies on the Russian River	41
Neighborhoods Are Not a Game	60
New Poem	113
No One Here	121
Now What?	88
Old Clocks	129
Old Images	46
On Grandma's Chair	126
On the Cable Line Road	27
Over the Wall	61
Paper Boy	5
Penicillin	32
Perhaps Then	105
Persistent Illusion	18
Pillow Talk	106
Poem on a Napkin	112
Poet Passes, A	112
Poetry Zoo	115
Poets' Show and Tell	120
Property Disposal	128

Questions About an Armless Boy	62
Ready or Not	135
Reclining Women	89
Reconstruction	113
Remember Bougainvillea	97
River Child	42
Rommel's Buried Treasure	33
Running in the Louvre	98
Sex Education	8
Shanghai, '48	16
Skulls	vii
Slender Colonel	29
Sometimes a Poem	114
Spitfire – San Francisco	6
Spotless	91
Sweet Water, Sweet Life	51
Swiss Army Knife	99
Taste of Poetry, The	119
Things of Value	910
Throw Out the Back Seat	64
Tilman Riemenschneider's Fingers	63
To Kill a Snake	3
Toy Top	127
Tuman (The Mist)	125
Under These Roofs	38
Universe Rewound	67
Walk on the Beach	49
What is it about Milwaukee, Wisconsin?	48
Where the Snowmen Go	138
Zinfandel Smile	102
Ziusudra, The Faraway (101)	66

www.ingramcontent.com/pod-product-compliance
Lightning Source LLC
Chambersburg PA
CBHW071402290426
44108CB00014B/1659